# A Child's First Library of Learning

# Pets

TIME-LIFE BOOKS • ALEXANDRIA, VIRGINIA

# Contents

How Can You Tell What Your Pet Is Feeling? . . . . . . . . . . . . . . . . . . . . . . . . . . . . .04

What Should You Name Your Pet? . . . . . . . . . . . . . . . . . . . . . . . . . . . . . . . . . . . .06

Can a Pet Catch a Cold? . . . . . . . . . . . . . . . . . . . . . . . . . . . . . . . . . . . . . . . . . . .08

What Does a Veterinarian Do? . . . . . . . . . . . . . . . . . . . . . . . . . . . . . . . . . . . . . . .10

How Old Do Pets Get? . . . . . . . . . . . . . . . . . . . . . . . . . . . . . . . . . . . . . . . . . . . . .12

What Is the Best Home for a Pet? . . . . . . . . . . . . . . . . . . . . . . . . . . . . . . . . . . . . .14

What Are Some of the Different Kinds of Dogs? . . . . . . . . . . . . . . . . . . . . . . . . . .16

How Smart Is Your Dog? . . . . . . . . . . . . . . . . . . . . . . . . . . . . . . . . . . . . . . . . . . . .18

How Do Dogs Help People? . . . . . . . . . . . . . . . . . . . . . . . . . . . . . . . . . . . . . . . . .20

How Can Dogs Hear Dog Whistles When We Don't Hear Anything? . . . . . . . . . . . .22

Why Do Dogs Turn Around in a Circle Before They Lie Down? . . . . . . . . . . . . . . . .24

How Should You Approach a Dog You Don't Know? . . . . . . . . . . . . . . . . . . . . . . . .26

What Is a Calico Cat? . . . . . . . . . . . . . . . . . . . . . . . . . . . . . . . . . . . . . . . . . . . . . .28

Can a Cat See in the Dark? . . . . . . . . . . . . . . . . . . . . . . . . . . . . . . . . . . . . . . . . . .30

Why Do Some People Think that Black Cats Bring Bad Luck? . . . . . . . . . . . . . . . . .32

How Many Different Kinds of Horses Are There? . . . . . . . . . . . . . . . . . . . . . . . . . .34

What Do You Need to Ride a Horse? . . . . . . . . . . . . . . . . . . . . . . . . . . . . . . . . . . .36

Do Horses Really Sleep Standing Up? . . . . . . . . . . . . . . . . . . . . . . . . . . . . . . . . . .38

Which Birds Can Talk? . . . . . . . . . . . . . . . . . . . . . . . . . . . . . . . . . . . . . . . . . . . . . .40

Why Do Birds Eat Pebbles? . . . . . . . . . . . . . . . . . . . . . . . . . . . . . . . . . . . . . . . . . .42

What Is the Best Home for a Fish? . . . . . . . . . . . . . . . . . . . . . . . . . . . . . . . . . . . . .44

Can Fish Drown? . . . . . . . . . . . . . . . . . . . . . . . . . . . . . . . . . . . . . . . . . . . . . . . . . . . . . .46
What Is a Reptile? . . . . . . . . . . . . . . . . . . . . . . . . . . . . . . . . . . . . . . . . . . . . . . . . . . . . .48
Can You Take a Lizard for a Walk? . . . . . . . . . . . . . . . . . . . . . . . . . . . . . . . . . . . . . .50
What Kinds of Turtles Make Good Pets? . . . . . . . . . . . . . . . . . . . . . . . . . . . . . . . .52
Can a Turtle Leave Its Shell? . . . . . . . . . . . . . . . . . . . . . . . . . . . . . . . . . . . . . . . . . .54
Why Do Snakes Shed Their Skin? . . . . . . . . . . . . . . . . . . . . . . . . . . . . . . . . . . . . .56
Where Can a Pet Frog Live? . . . . . . . . . . . . . . . . . . . . . . . . . . . . . . . . . . . . . . . . . .58
What Is a Rodent? . . . . . . . . . . . . . . . . . . . . . . . . . . . . . . . . . . . . . . . . . . . . . . . . . . .60
What Can a Pet Mouse or Rat Do? . . . . . . . . . . . . . . . . . . . . . . . . . . . . . . . . . . . .62
How Did the Guinea Pig Get Its Name? . . . . . . . . . . . . . . . . . . . . . . . . . . . . . . . .64
Why Do Hamsters Have Such Big Cheeks? . . . . . . . . . . . . . . . . . . . . . . . . . . . .66
Why Do Rabbits Thump Their Feet? . . . . . . . . . . . . . . . . . . . . . . . . . . . . . . . . . .68
Can Rabbits Be Housebroken? . . . . . . . . . . . . . . . . . . . . . . . . . . . . . . . . . . . . . . .70
Why Do Ferrets Smell So Bad? . . . . . . . . . . . . . . . . . . . . . . . . . . . . . . . . . . . . . . .72
Can an Insect Be a Pet? . . . . . . . . . . . . . . . . . . . . . . . . . . . . . . . . . . . . . . . . . . . . .74
Why Can't You Make a Pet Out of a Wild Animal? . . . . . . . . . . . . . . . . . . . . . .76
Can an Animal Have a Pet? . . . . . . . . . . . . . . . . . . . . . . . . . . . . . . . . . . . . . . . . . .78
What Kinds of Pets Are These? . . . . . . . . . . . . . . . . . . . . . . . . . . . . . . . . . . . . . . .80

Growing-Up Album . . . . . . . . . . . . . . . . . . . . . . . . . . . . . . . . . . . . . . . . . . . . . . . . .81

# How Can You Tell What Your Pet Is Feeling?

**ANSWER** Pets have feelings just like people do. Animals don't use words, but they can let you know what they are feeling by the sounds they make and by the way they act. Can you tell what these pets are trying to say?

**A happy dog**

When a dog is happy to see you, it will wag its tail and jump up and down excitedly. The dog may try to lick your face and bring you a toy as a way of asking you to play with it.

**A guilty-looking dog**

When a dog knows it has done something it shouldn't have, it will hide in a corner and will not look at you.

**A frisky cat**

A cat likes to play when it is happy. Even though it may pounce wildly or look very serious as it swats at a shoe or a piece of string, it's all in fun.

**A scared cat**

When a cat is scared, it tries to look bigger by fluffing up its fur and its tail; then it arches its back to look fierce and dangerous.

## ■ Looking for trouble

When a rabbit hears a noise, it will rise up on its hind legs, turn its ears toward the noise, and try to sniff out any danger that may be near. If the rabbit is scared by someone or something, it will thump a foot hard to tell the other rabbits to run away.

## ■ Bird buddies

Pet birds can become good friends. They like to play together and often help each other groom hard-to-reach places. Here one bird is helping its friend by cleaning the feathers on the back of its neck.

● **To the Parent**

When you teach your child that pets have feelings, you are encouraging him or her to have compassion and respect for animals. As your child tries to decipher what a pet needs and feels, by observing its body language and listening to the sounds it makes, your child is learning important communication lessons. A child and a pet can be great playmates and friends, and their friendship will grow deeper as they understand each other more. A pet may be one of your child's closest friends.

5

#  What Should You Name Your Pet?

 **ANSWER** You can name your pet whatever you like. If you call your pet by its name each time you play with your pet, it will learn to recognize its name. If you want to teach your dog to obey commands, make sure that you do not give it a name that sounds like "sit," "stay," or "heel," or your dog may get confused. For example, if you name your dog Ray, it may not know when you are calling it and when you want it to stay.

## ■ Pets with personality

Once you get to know your pet, its personality may give you an idea for the perfect name. Can you tell what these pets act like?

| Frisky | Bashful | Bruiser | Snoopy |
| Princess | Happy | Picky-Picky | Bandit |

## ■ See and say

You can name your pet by what it looks like. Special markings, the color of its fur, or the feel of its skin may help you think of a name that is just right.

Tiger

Fluffy

Spot

Tiny

Godzilla

Speedy

## ■ Funny names

You may want to give your pet a silly name. The pets shown here are named for opposites. The big dog is called Tiny, the slow turtle's name is Speedy, and the tiny mouse is named for a huge monster in the movies called Godzilla.

## ■ Famous pets

▲ The name of television star Lassie simply means girl.

◄ Socks belongs to President Clinton's daughter, Chelsea. The cat got its name from the white fur on its paws that looks like white socks.

7

# ? Can a Pet Catch a Cold?

**ANSWER** Pets can get sick the same way people do. If your pet is listless and does not want to eat, it may be sick. A sick cat sometimes looks as if it has a cold. Its eyes get watery and the third eyelids close halfway. The cat has a runny nose, and it does not want to play. Then it is time to take your cat to the veterinarian.

## ■ How to tell if your cat is sick

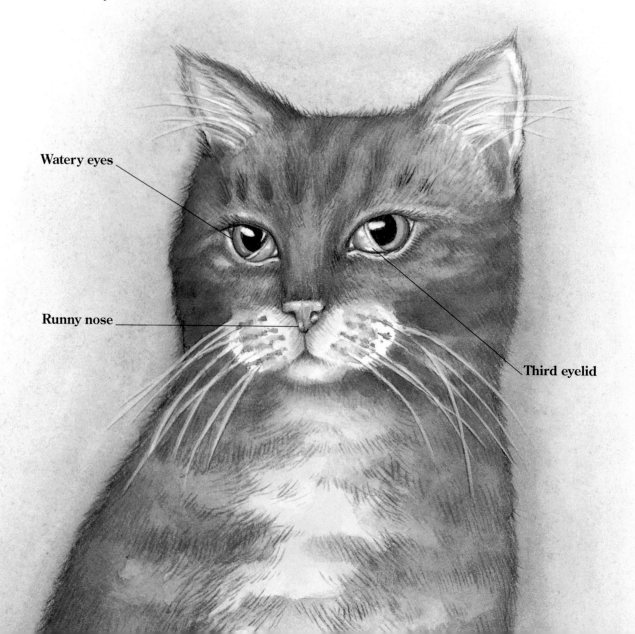

Watery eyes

Runny nose

Third eyelid

# Why Do Cats Make Some People Sneeze?

Some people are allergic to cats. When they are near a cat, their eyes begin to water, their nose runs, they sneeze, and they cough. Many people think it is the cat's hair that makes them sick, but it is really the cat's saliva. Cats clean themselves by licking their fur. Their saliva dries and tiny particles in it drift into the air. When people who are allergic breathe in these particles, they start to sneeze.

◄ **Bath time**
When a cat cleans itself, it licks its fur with its tongue again and again. For hard-to-reach places, the cat wets its paw and washes with it as if it were a washcloth.

● **To the Parent**

If you think the family pet is sick, or if it has been in an accident, take the animal to the veterinarian's office right away. A new pet should be checked out by a veterinarian and get all necessary vaccines. Some animals also need deworming. But your pet cannot catch the measles, or another illness, from a family member, and it would be unusual for you to catch a disease from a pet. Even so, you may avoid visits to the pediatrician if you make sure that your child washes his or her hands after playing with a pet.

# What Does a Veterinarian Do?

**ANSWER** A veterinarian is a doctor who takes care of pets and other animals. This doctor had to go to veterinary school to learn how to tell if an animal is sick, and how to make a sick or hurt animal well again. A veterinarian takes care of earaches and eye infections, fixes broken bones, and cures many other diseases.

## ■ A checkup for a pet

Even a healthy animal needs to go to the veterinarian for regular checkups. Here are some of the things the veterinarian may do during a checkup:

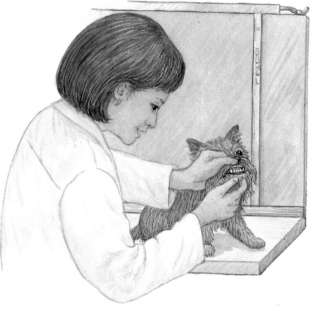

▲ The veterinarian also checks an animal's teeth. If an animal has a toothache, the vet knows how to fill a cavity or pull a tooth. The vet has to be the animal's doctor and dentist.

▲ The veterinarian will check your pet's eyes and ears to make sure the animal can see and hear without problems.

10

▼ The veterinarian will listen to the animal's heart and lungs with a stethoscope.

▲ The veterinarian may give your pet a shot to keep it from getting a disease, like rabies.

## ■ Operations and emergencies

▲ Sometimes there are emergencies. The veterinarian can mend the delicate bones in a bird's wing, take x-rays, or perform surgery.

## ■ Large animal veterinarian

Some veterinarians take care of farm animals, such as pigs, cows, sheep, horses, and other large animals. These doctors often make house calls, since it is not easy to bring a large animal to the vet's office.

● **To the Parent**

Veterinarians are trained to care for many different kinds of animals, from dogs and cats to exotic lizards and birds. Veterinarians do checkups, give shots, and perform surgery. Some veterinarians still make house calls. Many children think they want to become veterinarians when they grow up. Encourage your child to come along on a visit to observe the veterinarian's work.

# How Old Do Pets Get?

(ANSWER) Pets do not live as long as people do, but they grow up a lot faster than people. Even so, pets live for many years. It is important to think about how long you will need to care for a pet. Old pets may need special care, such as extra sleep or special food.

## ■ Watch them grow

Newborn kittens and puppies spend their first two weeks with their eyes closed. When they can see, they begin to walk on wobbly legs. They stay close to their mothers to be fed and kept warm. By the time they are six weeks old, they are ready to explore on their own. A foal can stand up right after it is born. When it is three months old, it will gallop around the field and play with other foals. At six months old it is as tall as its mother.

## Kitten

**3 weeks old**

**6 weeks old**

**18 weeks old**

## Puppy

**2 days old**

**2 weeks old**

**8 weeks old**

## ■ Oldest pets

▼ The oldest known cat, a female tabby named Ma, died when she was 34 years old.

▼ A guinea pig named Snowball beat all records by living to be 8 years and 4 ½ months old.

▲ The oldest dog on record was an Australian cattle dog named Bluey. He lived to be 29 years and 5 months old.

▲ The oldest caged bird was a parrot named Prudle, who lived to be 35 years old.

## Foal

½ hour old

3 months old

6 months old

## ■ Average life span

| | |
|---|---|
| Horse | 22 years |
| Cat | 14 years |
| Dog | 13 years |
| Goldfish | 10 years |
| Parakeet | 10 years |
| Guinea pig | 4 years |

# What Is the Best Home for a Pet?

**ANSWER** The best home for a pet is a place where it gets a lot of love and attention. If you care about your pet, you will make sure that it gets everything it needs. Remember that your pet counts on you to take care of it. Your fish cannot clean its own tank or find its own food. Here are some of the things every pet needs:

## ▼ Exercise

Exercise keeps your pet healthy and happy. Some pets, like fish, get enough exercise on their own. Other pets, such as dogs, need a big yard to run in. If you don't have a yard, you should take your dog for a long walk every day or play games with a Frisbee or a ball.

## ▲ Food

Make sure to feed your pet the right kind of food, in the amount the veterinarian suggests. Although some pets prefer people food, they will get a better diet if you feed them the pet food that is meant for them.

# ■ Cleanliness

◄ Some pets keep themselves clean, but others may need a bath. In summer you can bathe your dog outdoors. When it is cold you should wash it indoors, in the bathtub. Pets also need a clean place to live and sleep. You will have to clean out a hamster cage, birdcage, or fishbowl regularly. Remember that pets like birds and hamsters spend their whole lives in a small space; to keep them healthy you must keep their home clean.

## ■ Safety tips

Never leave your pet in a hot car in the summer, or outside for too long in the winter when it is cold.

Don't let your pet chew on toys that could be harmful if they break or if they are swallowed.

Make sure your pet does not chew on electrical cords or lap up any dangerous chemicals.

To avoid accidents, always keep your dog on a leash when you take it out for a walk.

### ► Water

Make sure that your pet can get a fresh drink of water whenever it is thirsty. The water in its dish must be changed every day.

### ◄ Holding your pet the right way

Pets get scared if they think they are going to fall, so make sure that you always hold the animal firmly, giving it lots of support. But be gentle when holding your pet; animals don't like to be squeezed. If your pet is struggling to get away from you, quickly put it back into its cage or set the dog or cat on the ground. Never drop your pet or let it fall.

# What Are Some of the Different Kinds of Dogs?

**ANSWER** There are more than 400 breeds, or kinds, of dogs. Most dog breeds fit into one of the six groups shown on these pages. Breeds that do not fit into one of these groups are in the nonsporting group.

▼ **Terrier group**
The Airedale is one of the largest terriers. They are good hunters. Other terriers were bred to rout rats out of their hiding places.

◀ **Toy group**
The small dogs in the toy group, like the Bichon Frise *(left)*, were bred to be good pets.

**Dogs on Parade**

**Belgian Shepherd**
*Herding group*

**Pharaoh Hound**
*Hound group*

**Boxer**
*Working group*

16

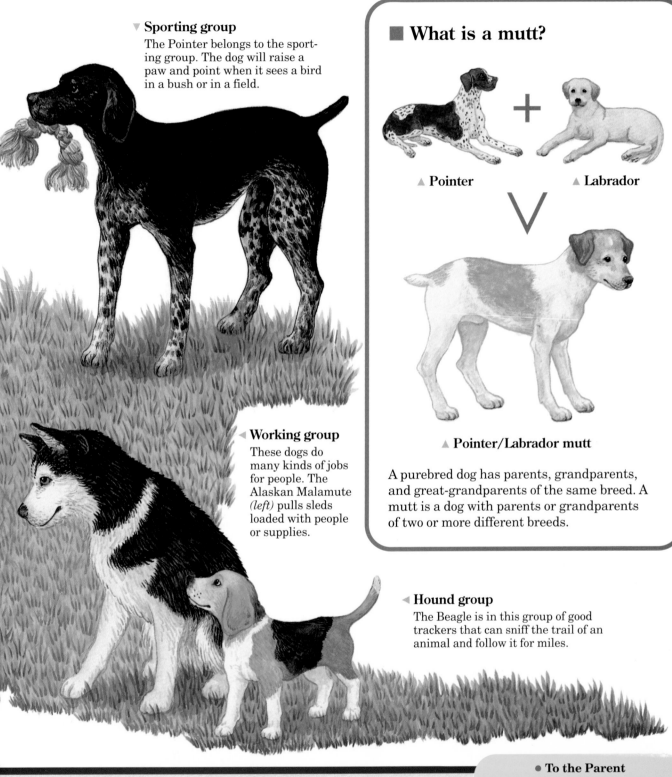

## ▼ Sporting group

The Pointer belongs to the sporting group. The dog will raise a paw and point when it sees a bird in a bush or in a field.

### ■ What is a mutt?

▲ Pointer     ▲ Labrador

▲ Pointer/Labrador mutt

A purebred dog has parents, grandparents, and great-grandparents of the same breed. A mutt is a dog with parents or grandparents of two or more different breeds.

### ◄ Working group

These dogs do many kinds of jobs for people. The Alaskan Malamute *(left)* pulls sleds loaded with people or supplies.

### ◄ Hound group

The Beagle is in this group of good trackers that can sniff the trail of an animal and follow it for miles.

**Old English Sheepdog**
*Herding group*

**Whippet**
*Hound group*

● To the Parent

Dogs come in an amazing variety of shapes, sizes, and colors—from the tiny Chihuahua to the massive Mastiff, and from the hairy Puli to the Peruvian Hairless. Some of these breeds are shown along the bottom of these and the following pages, through page 27.

# ❓ How Smart Is Your Dog?

**ANSWER** A dog cannot read a book or do math problems. But that does not mean your dog is dumb. A dog can be judged by human standards, by how fast it learns to obey a command like "sit" or "heel" and by how well it can learn a job that helps people. A dog can also be judged by animal skills, by how easily it can find food or a comfortable place to lie in. The dogs described on these pages are smart by any standards.

**Dogs on Parade**

**Bullmastiff**
*Working group*

**Poodle**
*Nonsporting group*

**Chihuahua**
*Toy group*

**Greyhound**
*Hound group*

## ■ Tasha to the rescue

Tasha and her newborn puppies lived in a yard
with a locked fence around it. When the area
flooded with water, Tasha could not carry all
her puppies in her mouth, as she normally
would, to save them. So, she put her puppies in her food dish and held it above
water until her owners arrived.

## ■ Dogs save the day

Dogs have saved many peo-
ple from getting burned in
a fire by barking loudly
and waking them up. The
Aurora Fire Department in
Colorado gave Dakota, a black
Labrador, a medal for valor.
She woke up her owners so
they could get out of their
burning house safely.

● **To the Parent**

There are various kinds of intelli-
gence among dogs, depending on
the breed and their training. Encourage your child to respect the
abilities and skills of the family
dog. Many dogs have shown amazing bravery in the face of danger
and have saved people from per-
ilous situations.

**Afghan Hound**
*Hound group*

**Bearded Collie**
*Herding group*

**Pekingese**
*Toy group*

19

# How Do Dogs Help People?

(ANSWER) Your dog probably has only one job—being your friend. Most pet dogs also guard their family by barking loudly to frighten away a stranger. Other dogs have been trained to guide the blind, pull a sled in the snow, or search for people and rescue them.

## ■ Herding dogs

Herding dogs will run with a flock of sheep or a herd of cattle and keep any of the animals from getting lost.

---

**Dogs on Parade**

**St. Bernard**
*Working group*

**Chinese Crested Dog**
*Toy group*

**Chow Chow**
*Nonsporting group*

▲ **Police dogs.** This Labrador Retriever helps the police by sniffing out illegal drugs or bombs. Police dogs also help find a missing person by following that person's scent.

▲ **Service dogs.** Some dogs are trained to help people who cannot use their arms or legs. This black Labrador carries things for his friend. Do not pet a service dog; it has to work.

## ■ Out of work

Before there were fire trucks, Dalmatians would run ahead of horse-drawn fire wagons and bark to warn people to get out of the way. When fire departments began using motorized fire trucks, dogs could no longer run with them. Some fire departments still keep Dalmatians as mascots.

**Weimaraner**
*Sporting group*

**Pug**
*Toy group*

**Puli**
*Herding group*

# How Can Dogs Hear Dog Whistles When We Don't Hear Anything?

**ANSWER** Dogs have better ears than humans. They can hear lower- and higher-pitched sounds than we can hear. A dog whistle makes a high-pitched sound that is out of the range of human hearing, but dogs can still hear it.

Dog whistle

Low pitch     Medium pitch     High pitch

## ■ Quiet call

A dog that has been trained to respond to a dog whistle will come running back to its owner, but people cannot hear the call.

---

**Dogs on Parade**

**Labrador Retriever**
*Sporting group*

**Shetland Sheepdog**
*Herding group*

**Dachshund**
*Hound group*

### ◀ Special ears

Dogs have 17 separate muscles in their ears. They can move their ears toward a sound to hear it better. They can even turn their ears in two different directions at once.

### ■ The nose knows

▲ Smell is one of a dog's most important senses. Dogs can smell who among their friends has walked before them and follow a scent to help find missing persons.

 ## Can Animals Predict Earthquakes?

Horses, cats, birds, fish, and a few other animals may act odd and excited before an earthquake. It could be that they pick up very small vibrations in the earth before humans notice them, at the beginning of an earthquake.

**Skye Terrier**
*Terrier group*

**Collie**
*Herding group*

# ❓ Why Do Dogs Turn Around in a Circle Before They Lie Down?

**(ANSWER)** Before dogs became pets thousands of years ago, they lived in the wild. When they wanted to go to sleep, they would find a grassy spot and walk around in a circle to stamp down the grass to make a bed. Today, pet dogs still stamp the ground, even though their bed may be a blanket or another soft spot in the house.

## ■ Living in packs

The dog's wild ancestors lived in groups, called packs. Members of the pack treated the leader of the pack with respect by licking its face. Today, pet dogs treat the humans they live with as members of their pack. When your dog licks your face, it may be because it thinks of you as the leader of the pack.

**Dogs on Parade**

**Bulldog**
*Nonsporting group*

**Peruvian Hairless**
*Nonsporting group*

**Rottweiler**
*Working group*

## ■ Messy houseguests

The dog's wild ancestors did not stay in one place for long. They did not care about keeping their house clean, because they knew they would be moving soon. Since a pet dog will be staying in the same house (your house!) for a long time, it is best to teach your dog to go to the bathroom on newspapers or outside.

## ■ In a hurry

In the wild a dog had to eat fast, or others in the pack would take its dinner. Today, the pet dog's instincts still tell it to eat rapidly and to snap and growl at anyone who comes near its food.

**Cocker Spaniel**
*Sporting group*

**Basset Hound**
*Hound group*

● **To the Parent**

As wild animals, dogs lived in packs. Domesticated dogs have kept certain behaviors that helped them in the wild. Snarling at intruders, gulping down their food-- these are the same instincts that tell a dog to bury a bone. The dog is trying to store food away to ensure that it will have enough food later.

# ❓ How Should You Approach a Dog You Don't Know?

**ANSWER** Some dogs are friendly with strangers and others are not. When you meet a dog you don't know, first find out if the dog wants to meet you, too. You should ask the dog's owner if the dog is friendly and if you can pet it. In most cases you can see for yourself whether the dog acts friendly, but always be careful.

## ■ Meeting a friendly dog

A friendly dog will wag its tail or jump up and down to greet you. The dog may try to roll over so you can scratch its stomach. Even friendly dogs need a little bit of time to decide if they trust you or not.

▶ Don't stare at the dog. Act calm and friendly. Let the dog come to you and smell your hand with the palm up.

▼ If the dog looks as if it wants to meet you, you can pet it.

**Dogs on Parade**

**Siberian Husky**
*Working group*

**Samoyed**
*Working group*

**Yorkshire Terrier**
*Toy group*

**Lowchen**
*Toy group*

# ■ Meeting an unfriendly dog

An unfriendly dog will growl to warn you not to come near. It may bark at you and stand with its legs stiff and its tail straight up. Stand still, don't stare at the dog or act scared, and let the dog sniff you. Most likely it will walk away once it has decided you are not a threat. Or you can walk away slowly. Don't run, or the dog will try to chase you.

# ■ Keep in mind

Many dogs will act unfriendly if they are protecting their territory, their master, or themselves. You can avoid being bitten by a dog if you:

- never tease a dog
- never disturb a dog while it is eating
- never wake a sleeping dog
- never hit a dog

**Boston Terrier**
*Nonsporting group*

**Pomeranian**
*Toy group*

**Great Dane**
*Working group*

● **To the Parent**

Children are involved in 60 percent of all dog bites. To keep your child from getting bitten, teach your child never to disturb a dog while it is eating or sleeping, and never to tease a dog. A dog chained up outside will protect its territory and may bite a trespasser even though it may be friendly inside the house.

#  What Is a Calico Cat?

**ANSWER** Cats come in many colors. A calico cat's fur is colored with patches of black, orange, and white, like calico patchwork. It is different from the coat of a tortoiseshell cat, whose fur has the same colors all mixed together. Both of these cats share an odd trait: They are almost always female.

▼ **Tortoiseshell**
These multicolored cats are sometimes called torties.

## ■ Different breeds

▶ **Siamese**
The slender Siamese have blue eyes and dark markings on their faces, legs, and tails. Their loud voices can sound like a crying baby.

▲ **Persian**
Persian cats have round faces and long, soft fur. Their long hair should be brushed every day so it will not get matted.

## ■ The cat without a tail

Manx cats don't have a tail. They come from the Isle of Man, an island off the coast of England. They have lived there for hundreds of years. The first cat without a tail may have come to the island on a ship. That cat then had kittens without tails, who had more kittens without tails—and soon the island was full of Manx cats.

Cats shed their fur all year round. If you don't brush your cat often, much of its loose hair will end up on you.

**► Sphinx**
Looking mysterious, like an Egyptian sphinx, these strange cats have almost no hair.

**► Angora**
These cats have thick, silky hair and long tails. They come from Turkey, where they were once the favorite pets of kings.

**● To the Parent**

The reason why calico and tortoise-shell cats are almost always female is genetics. A cat needs two X chromosomes to have black and orange fur coloring, one carrying the gene for black fur and one carrying the gene for orange fur. Because a cat with two X chromosomes must be a female, cats with both black and orange coloring are female.

29

#  Can a Cat See in the Dark?

**ANSWER** A cat cannot see in total darkness, but it can see better at night than many animals, including humans. A kind of mirror at the back of a cat's eye collects every last bit of light. So, when there is only a little light, cats can see more than people can. Light enters a cat's eye through its pupil. When it is dark, the pupils open wide. In bright light, they turn into narrow slits.

▲ Cats' eyes glow in the dark. They glow because of cells at the back of the eyes, which form a kind of mirror that reflects light back. The reflection helps cats see at night.

## ■ Cats' eyes

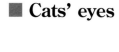

**At night**

**On a cloudy day**

**On a sunny day**

▼ **Taking a catnap**

◄ **In a deep sleep**

Cats spend a lot of time catnapping, or lightly sleeping, with their eyes half-closed. When they go into a deep sleep, they close their upper and lower eyelids, and the thin third eyelids *(see page 8)*.

30

# Why Does My Cat Act the Way It Does?

Cats pounce on things to practice their hunting skills. When they play with toys, they are also pretending to hunt. Cats lick their fur with their rough tongues to remove dirt and loose hairs. They may scratch furniture to remove the dead outer covering of their claws.

▼ **Pouncing**

**Sleeping**

▼ **Balancing**

Cats walk on narrow rails and tree limbs, keeping perfect balance. They use their legs and claws to keep themselves from falling.

▽ **Scratching**

**Cleaning**

**Playing**

**Marking territory**

A cat rubs against things and people to leave its mark. Other cats can tell by the smell of the mark which cat was there. The cat is telling other cats that "this is mine."

# Why Do Some People Think that Black Cats Bring Bad Luck?

**ANSWER** During the Middle Ages, people thought black cats were witches in disguise. So whenever they saw an all-black cat, they worried that it might cast a bad spell on them. In some places people think black cats bring good luck. In England some people say that if a black cat strays into their home, they will soon receive money.

**▲ Rain or shine?**
Some people think that cats can predict the weather. They say: If a cat sneezes, it's going to rain; if a cat runs crazily around the house, it's going to be windy.

In some parts of the world, people believe that if a black cat crosses in front of them, a wish will come true. But other people think that having a black cat cross in front of them means they will have bad luck that day.

# Do Cats Really Have Nine Lives?

No, cats have one life, like every other creature. But cats can survive falls from great heights that would kill other animals. A long time ago, people who watched such falls believed cats had magical powers that made it possible for them to come back to life after they died. Because nine was thought to be a lucky number, people said that any animal fortunate enough to have more than one life would surely have nine of them.

▲ Even if a cat falls from an upside-down position, it can turn itself during the fall to land on its feet. But it is not always safe for cats to fall. Cats can get hurt when they are dropped.

## ■ A cat-goddess

The ancient Egyptians believed cats were the helpers of Bastet, the cat-headed goddess of motherhood. They kept statues of Bastet in their homes. When a cat died, it was wrapped up as a mummy and buried in a tomb, along with a saucer of milk.

### ● To the Parent

For millennia, people around the world treated cats as prized pets, sometimes even elevating them to divine status. Ancient Egyptians worshiped the cat-goddess Bastet. Buddhist myth holds that cats become the temporary resting place for the soul of some deeply spiritual people. During the Middle Ages in Europe, attitudes toward cats changed radically when cats were associated with witches and black magic. Not until the 17th century did people welcome cats back into their households as gentle companions—and as useful rodent controllers.

# How Many Different Kinds of Horses Are There?

**ANSWER** About 150 different breeds of horses exist in the world today. Some horses are a mixture of several breeds. They are called crossbreeds. Horses come in many different sizes and colors. The most common colors for horses are brown, chestnut (reddishbrown), black, and gray.

**▲ Thoroughbred**
The Thoroughbred is a strong, fast horse. It can run up to 40 miles an hour for short distances. This speed makes it a good horse for racing, hunting, and playing polo, a game of skill on horseback.

**▼ Mustang**
Long ago, Native Americans tamed wild mustangs roaming the West and used them to hunt for buffalo.

**▲ Arabian**
Arabian horses are prized for their strength and endurance in the deserts of North Africa. People have been riding horses there for 3,000 years.

**▲ Clydesdale**
This horse first came from Scotland, where it was used to pull heavy loads. Its big feet are topped with thick tufts of hair, called feathering.

**► American Quarter Horse**
This horse can go from a halt to a gallop very quickly. It also can run for a long time. Cowboys like to ride these horses to herd cattle and to compete in rodeos.

# What Is a Pony?

Some breeds of horses are smaller than average. They are called ponies. A horse's height is measured in "hands." One hand is about four inches, or the width of the palm of an average adult. Any horse that is shorter than 14.2 hands (57 inches) is called a pony.

▲ **Shetland Pony**
This shaggy pony is known for being gentle, although it is strong and can carry heavy loads on its back. It comes from the Shetland Islands of Scotland, from which it got its name.

## ■ World's smallest horse

◀ Miniature horses are even smaller than ponies. They are no taller than 8.5 hands, or 34 inches. This newborn "mini," which is only 15 inches tall and weighs 24 pounds, is small enough to carry.

## ■ Measuring a horse

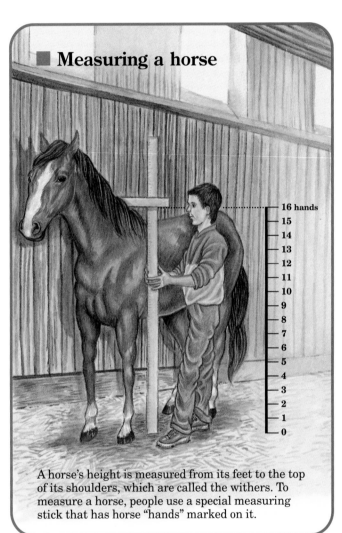

16 hands
15
14
13
12
11
10
9
8
7
6
5
4
3
2
1
0

A horse's height is measured from its feet to the top of its shoulders, which are called the withers. To measure a horse, people use a special measuring stick that has horse "hands" marked on it.

# ? What Do You Need to Ride a Horse?

**ANSWER** To ride a horse safely and easily, you have to outfit your horse with some basic equipment known as tack. You will need a bridle and bit with reins to help you control the horse. You also should have a saddle with stirrups to make your ride more comfortable. It takes practice to learn how to put tack on and take it off.

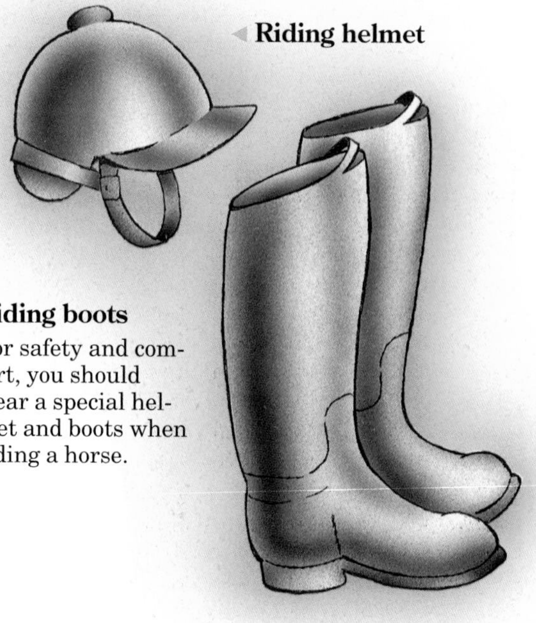

◀ **Riding helmet**

▶ **Riding boots**
For safety and comfort, you should wear a special helmet and boots when riding a horse.

## ■ Basic tack

The bridle and the bit control the horse's head. The reins attached to the bridle help you change direction or slow the horse down. The saddle and stirrups let you sit securely.

**Bridle**

**Bit**

**Saddle**

**Reins**

**Stirrups**

# Why Do Horses Need Shoes?

Horses, like people, need shoes to protect their feet, or hoofs. Sometimes the horseshoes help correct a problem with the horse's hoofs or legs. Horseshoes are made of metal. Horses should have their feet checked every six weeks to make sure the shoes still fit right.

## ■ Horseshoeing

▲ Horseshoes are nailed into a horse's hoofs. But the nails do not hurt the horse, because the hoofs are made of keratin, which is the same material that human fingernails are made of. Hoofs, like fingernails, can be cut without causing any pain.

**MINI-DATA**

In the Middle Ages, knights in armor could not move well enough to climb on a horse. They had to be lifted onto their horses with a winch.

● **To the Parent**

There are two main categories of saddles: English and Western. The English saddle, shown opposite, is flatter than the Western saddle and does not have the Western's characteristic horn. Which saddle your child uses will depend not as much on where you live as on what kind of riding your child wants to do. If your child wants to learn to jump, for example, you will need an English saddle.

37

#  Do Horses Really Sleep Standing Up?

(ANSWER) Yes, horses sleep for about eight hours every day. They doze standing up for most of that time. But horses also lie down at night, when nobody sees them. Then they sleep for about two hours. Sometimes during this deep sleep they are dreaming.

## ■ Dozing

A horse sleeps standing up because it feels safer that way. If danger comes, the horse can wake up quickly, and without wasting time getting up on its feet, it can run away.

## ■ Deep sleep

A horse goes into a deep sleep when it is lying down. It sleeps on its side with all four legs stretched out.

# How Do Other Animals Sleep?

◄ Before going to
sleep, a parakeet
fluffs up its feath-
ers, tucks its head
under a wing, and
closes its eyes.

▼ Wild rabbits sleep during the
day in their underground
homes. They come out at night
to eat and play.

▶ Snakes sleep
curled up in a
safe hiding place.
They sleep with
their eyes open;
they have no eye-
lids to close.

▲ Fish sleep by keeping perfectly still,
hidden among water plants or in the
mud at the bottom of a lake. Like
snakes, fish have no eyelids. Their
eyes stay open while they rest.

**MINI-DATA**

Wild horses take turns sleeping. One or two horses stay awake
and watch out for danger, while the others rest or sleep.

● **To the Parent**

To stay healthy, pets need the same
day-night cycle they would experi-
ence in their natural environment.
Exotic birds, fish, and other pets
from tropical climates, where day
and night are each 12 hours long
all year round, benefit the most
from controlled lighting. Turn off
all lights near your pet's cage or
tank during this rest period.

# Which Birds Can Talk?

**ANSWER** Birds cannot "talk." But some birds are good mimics. They can imitate many sounds, including human speech. The best talkers are parrots, parakeets, and other hook-billed birds. Hookbills have a short, curved beak, a thick tongue, and claws. But the myna, which is a soft-billed bird, is also a good mimic. It speaks very clearly and is great at whistling.

▲ **Polly want a cracker?**
Sometimes the promise of a treat will make your bird try harder to talk.

◀ **African Gray Parrot**
The best talking birds are the African Gray parrots. Some of these Parrots can learn to "speak" hundreds of different words.

▶ **Parakeet**
Some parakeets become great talkers. One parakeet raised in England learned to recite eight nursery rhymes.

▲ **Greater Hill Myna**
These birds are great mimics. They can imitate all kinds of sounds, from the ring of a telephone to the bark of a dog.

## ■ How to teach your bird to talk

Start by saying a simple word to your bird, like "hello," "cocoa," or "goodie," over and over again. Then repeat it three or four times a day. When your bird knows that word, you can teach it to say your address or telephone number. If your bird gets lost, it can "tell" the people who find it how to contact you.

▼ **Macaw**
These are very smart birds. They can learn to do tricks as well as speak. Macaws live a long time. Some pet macaws have lived to be more than 100 years old.

◄ **Cockatiel**
These birds come from Australia. They are quiet, gentle birds, but they can learn to say many words.

## ■ Other popular birds

Talking birds are not the only birds that make good pets. Many people like to have birds with colorful feathers, or a fanciful crest, or those that sing beautiful melodies in their homes.

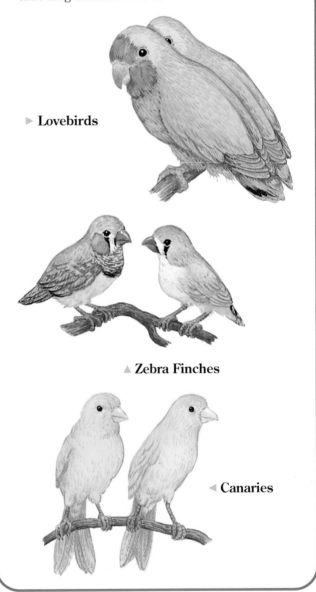

► **Lovebirds**

▲ **Zebra Finches**

◄ **Canaries**

# ⟨?⟩ Why Do Birds Eat Pebbles?

**ANSWER** Birds don't have any teeth. They cannot chew their food before it goes into their stomachs. But food needs to be broken up before it can be digested. To help their stomachs grind up food, birds eat very small pebbles known as grit. Your veterinarian will tell you how often you should feed your bird some grit.

## ◼ A home for your parakeet

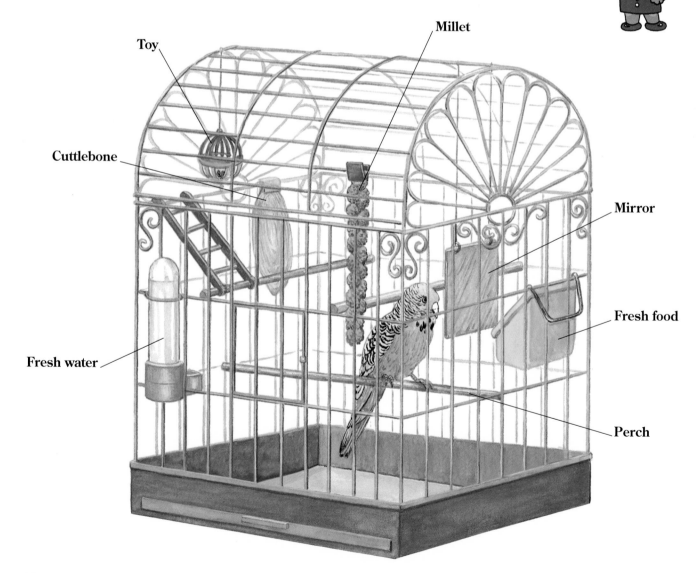

Toy

Millet

Cuttlebone

Mirror

Fresh food

Fresh water

Perch

42

# How Do They Keep Their Beaks Sharp?

A bird's beak is always growing. If the beak grows too long, the bird can have trouble eating. To keep your bird's beak from getting too big, put a cuttlebone in its cage. Your bird will sharpen its beak against the bone. While it is grooming its beak, your bird will also break off and eat tiny flakes of the bone. The bone contains minerals your bird needs.

## ■ Different beaks for different foods

The size and shape of a bird's beak can tell you what kind of food that bird eats in the wild. Some birds dig for insects and worms, others pick on fruit and berries, and a third group drinks only nectar from flowers.

▼ **Nectar drinker**
The sunbill's long, curved beak helps it get nectar from flowers.

◀ **Insect eater**
The Melba Finch's short, strong beak lets it dig into termite mounds and eat the insects.

▲ **Fruit eater**
No one knows for sure why the toucan has such a large beak, but it seems to help the bird get fruit from hard-to-reach tree branches.

● **To the Parent**

You can help your birds keep their beaks healthy and in shape. Make sure they have several dry, clean wood perches of various sizes. Birds like to clean their beaks on them after they eat. You should also provide them with dry, natural tree branches. Birds like to gnaw on those branches. Parrots, parakeets, and other hook-billed birds are particularly fond of chewing on wood and need a steady supply. Sometimes parakeet beaks become overgrown and need to be trimmed by an avian veterinarian or technician.

# What Is the Best Home for a Fish?

**ANSWER** Pet fish need a home that is as close to their natural environment as possible. Fish from cold waters should live in a cold-water tank. Fish from tropical waters need a heated tank. The tank should be lined with a layer of gravel. Plants will supply needed oxygen and give the fish a place to hide and rest.

## ■ Cold-water tank

Not all fish get along with each other. Goldfish and the other fish shown below can live together in an unheated tank and are the easiest to keep.

▲ **Saltwater tank**

A sea horse does not look like a fish, but it is a true fish with gills and fins. This graceful animal is difficult to keep at home: It needs a tank with running seawater.

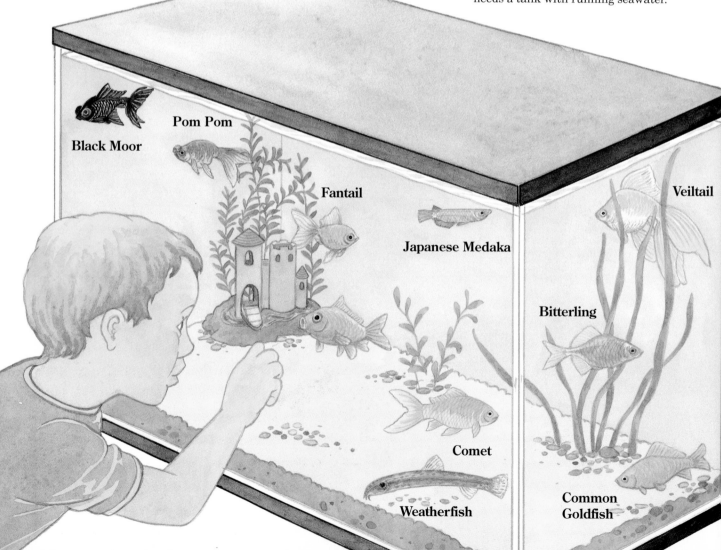

Black Moor

Pom Pom

Fantail

Japanese Medaka

Veiltail

Bitterling

Comet

Weatherfish

Common Goldfish

## ■ Warm-water tank

**Sunset Platy**

Warm-water fish need to live in a heated tank. The colorful fish shown here can all live together in a warm-water tank.

**Zebra Danio**

**Angelfish**

**Guppy**

**Rosy Barb**

**Swordtail**

**Black Molly**

**Leopard Corydorus**

## ■ Backyard pond

Some people keep fish in outdoor ponds. A popular fish for a backyard pond is the Japanese Koi. These carp can live outdoors all year round, even during ice-cold winters.

# Can Fish Drown?

**ANSWER** Yes, sometimes fish can drown. Like all animals, including humans, fish need to breathe oxygen to live. Oxygen is a gas that is in air and in water. Fish use their gills to breathe oxygen from water. People breathe oxygen from air. When people drown, it is because, without gills, water instead of oxygen gets into their lungs. When a fish drowns, it is because it cannot get enough oxygen from the water. That happens when the water is dirty.

## ■ The right environment for fish

Gill

Fish need clean, fresh water with oxygen in it. Some oxygen gets into the water from the air. Green plants that live in water also give out oxygen. The water in a fishtank must be changed regularly to make sure the pet fish have the right amount of oxygen.

# What Do Fish Eat?

In the wild, fish eat many different kinds of food. Some fish eat only plants. Others eat tiny insects that live on the water's surface, or they snack on worms that hide in the mud at the bottom. Many fish hunt and eat snails, frogs, and even other fish. Most fish kept in tanks can live on dried food flakes or pellets that are specially made for pet fish. When buying fish food, make sure it is the right kind for the fish in your tank.

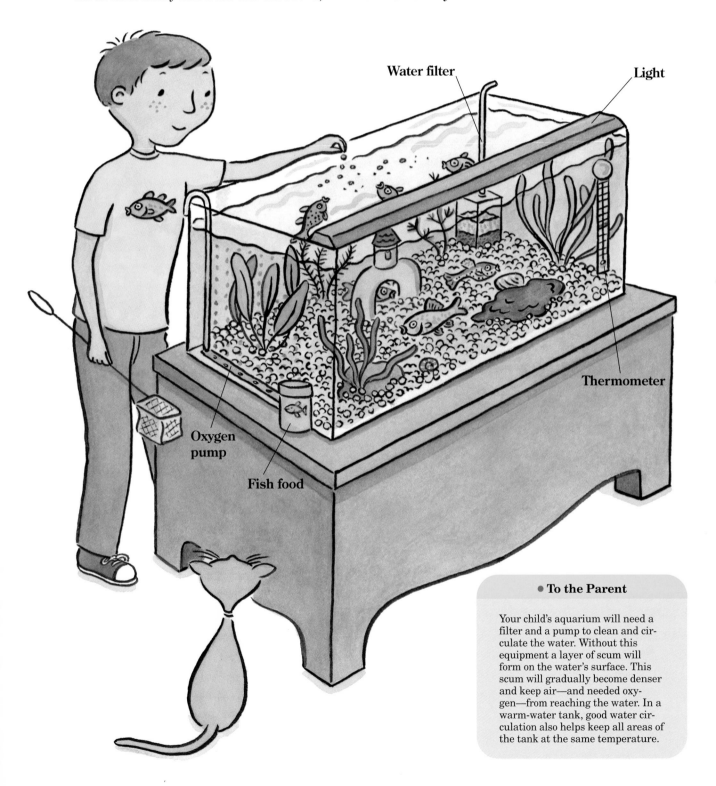

Water filter

Light

Thermometer

Oxygen pump

Fish food

● **To the Parent**

Your child's aquarium will need a filter and a pump to clean and circulate the water. Without this equipment a layer of scum will form on the water's surface. This scum will gradually become denser and keep air—and needed oxygen—from reaching the water. In a warm-water tank, good water circulation also helps keep all areas of the tank at the same temperature.

# ❓ What Is a Reptile?

**ANSWER** Reptiles are cold-blooded animals. The temperature inside their bodies is always about the same as the air or water temperature outside their bodies. They have backbones and thick, dry skin that is made up of either scales or bony plates. Not all reptiles have feet, but those that do, have claws. Lizards, snakes, crocodiles, alligators, and turtles are all reptiles.

■ **Desert environment**

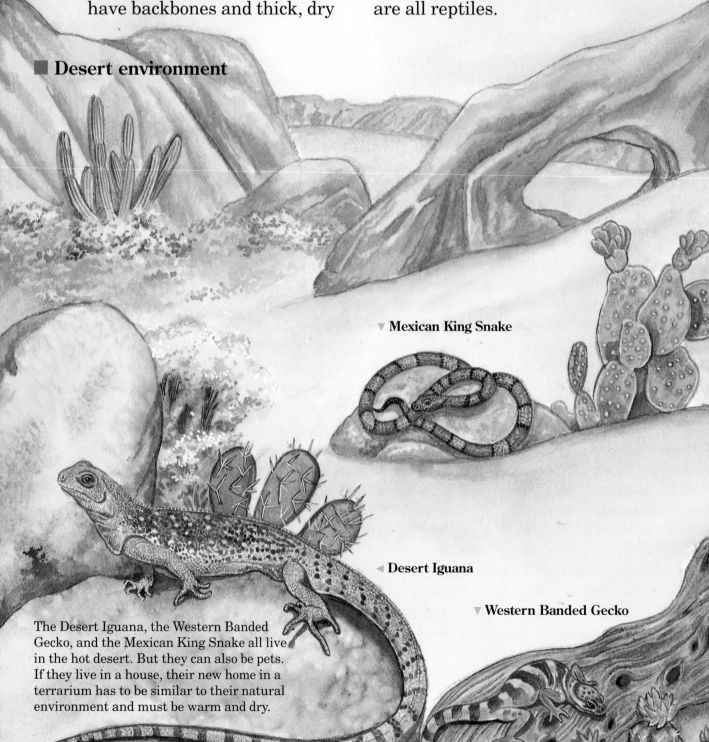

▼ **Mexican King Snake**

◄ **Desert Iguana**

▼ **Western Banded Gecko**

The Desert Iguana, the Western Banded Gecko, and the Mexican King Snake all live in the hot desert. But they can also be pets. If they live in a house, their new home in a terrarium has to be similar to their natural environment and must be warm and dry.

## ■ Wetlands environment

Some reptiles live in wetlands, the area where land and water meet. Wetlands lizards and turtles need a place to swim if they are kept as pets at home. Alligators are not pets; they are too dangerous and too large.

**Alligator**

## ■ Are reptiles good pets?

Reptiles are good pets for people who are allergic to animal hair. Reptile skin has no hair. But not all reptiles make good pets. Even if you have heard of baby alligators in homes, they are not pets. They bite and grow too large to keep at home. Other rare reptiles should be left to live in their natural environment. And most reptiles have needs that make them difficult to keep as pets.

**Diamondback Terrapin**

● **To the Parent**

Many reptiles face extinction, caused in part by the destruction of their natural habitats. In some parts of the world, reptiles are also hunted for their valuable skins. Thousands of rare reptiles have been sold illegally into the pet trade. Before buying a reptile, make sure it is not a threatened or endangered species. Buy only from reputable pet stores or dealers.

49

# ? Can You Take a Lizard for a Walk?

**ANSWER** Some people like to take their pet lizard for a walk. They use a special harness with a leash. But that is not a good idea. The lizards often break a leg or lose their tail. Although the tail can grow back, it may be a serious injury. A lizard should be kept safe in a terrarium that is similar to its natural environment.

Walking a lizard may look like fun, but your lizard is better off in its terrarium.

## Green iguana

The green iguana looks like a little dinosaur. When it is small, you can set up a perfect home for this pet lizard in an old fishtank. Some rocks and logs give it a place to hide.

A heat lamp helps keep the iguana warm. A special fluorescent lamp mimics sunlight to strengthen the iguana's bones and give this reptile's skin its healthy green color.

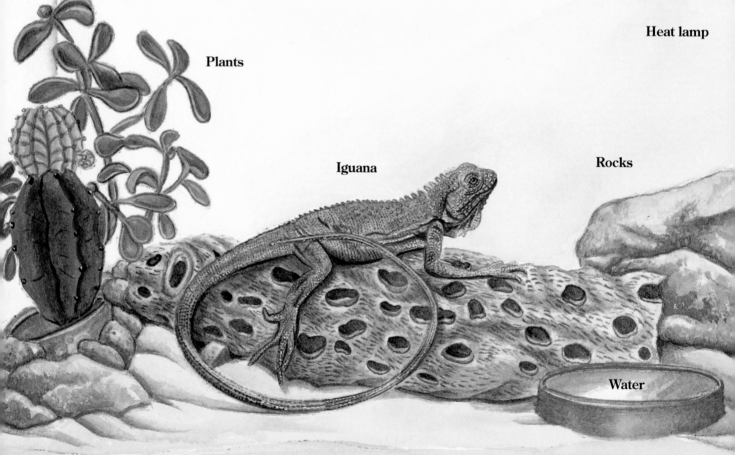

Plants

Heat lamp

Iguana

Rocks

Water

50

# What Are Some Types of Pet Lizards?

The green iguana may be the most popular lizard, but other types are often kept as pets, too. In many cases these rare animals need a lot of special care if they are to stay healthy.

▼ **Tokay Gecko**
The Tokay is one of the most popular pet geckos. Owners must handle it very carefully since it may bite.

▶ **Yemen Chameleon**
These amazing lizards change colors. They move slowly, but they have a quick tongue for catching insects.

▼ **Blue-Tongued Skink**
This robust lizard looks a bit like a snake with legs. Some pet owners feed their skinks cat or dog food.

▲ A gecko's toes stick to smooth surfaces. It can walk on the walls and even the ceiling of its glass cage.

# What Kinds of Turtles Make Good Pets?

**ANSWER** In the wild, some turtles live on land and others live in water. Turtles that live on land are easier to keep as pets. They can be kept in a dry terrarium. Water turtles need large water tanks. The water must be heated to just the right temperature and must be changed every other day. But if you are willing to care for a water turtle, it can make a great pet, too.

◀ **Eastern Box Turtle**

This colorful turtle lives mostly on land. Box Turtles are favorite pets and can learn to come to the sound of their name. Some live to be more than 100 years old.

▼ **Red-Eared Slider**

This water turtle gets its name from the red stripe by its ear. It grows to be about eight inches long.

▶ **Leopard Turtle**

This large land turtle is spotted like a leopard. It likes to eat fruit and vegetables. Some grow to be two feet long.

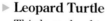

◀ **Painted Turtle**

This small water turtle does not mind cool temperatures during the winter.

52

# What Is a Turtle and What Is a Tortoise?

A turtle is any reptile with a shell. A tortoise is a turtle that spends its entire life on land. Most water turtles have webbed feet to help them swim. Most tortoises have short, stumpy legs to walk on land. A tortoise cannot swim well. It will drown in deep water.

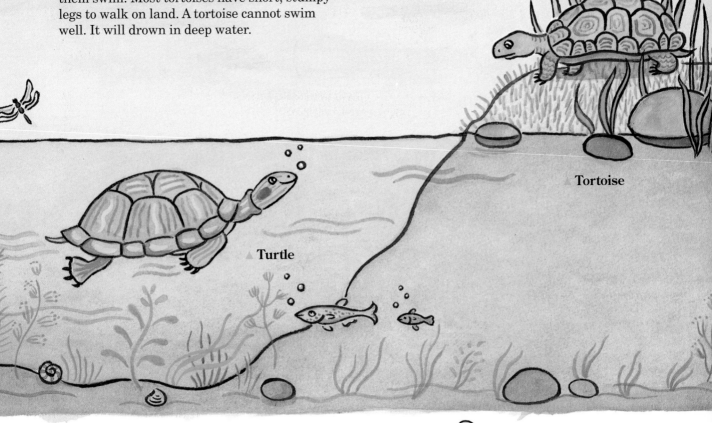

Tortoise

▲ Turtle

## ■ The largest pet turtle

▲ The African Spur-Thighed Tortoise often grows to four feet. During warm weather, it can be kept in the backyard. These turtles like to dig and bask in the sun.

# Can a Turtle Leave Its Shell?

(ANSWER) Unlike the hermit crab at right, a turtle cannot leave its shell. The shell is part of the turtle's skeleton, and it is also the turtle's home. The hard, bony shell protects the turtle from its enemies and bad weather. Water turtles have flatter shells than tortoises. The flatter shell makes it easier for the turtle to move through water.

## Carapace

Turtle shells have two main parts. The part that covers the turtle's back is called the carapace. It is made of horny plates, called scutes.

## Plastron

The part of the shell that covers the turtle's stomach is called the plastron. The plastron and the carapace are joined at the turtle's sides.

# Are Turtles Shy?

Turtles are careful creatures. When they sense danger, they quickly pull their head, tail, and legs into their shell. Sometimes they hiss like a snake. When a turtle pulls into its shell, it is telling you that it is frightened and wants to be left alone. You should respect the turtle's wishes and put it back in its terrarium and not try to make it come out again.

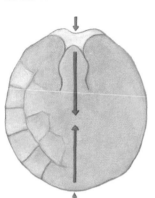

▲ Some turtles move their neck straight back when they pull it into their shell.

▲ Other turtles bend their neck to the side when they pull it into their shell.

◀ **How turtles hide inside**
Turtles fall into two groups: hidden-necked turtles and side-necked turtles. The hidden-necked turtle pulls its head straight back into the shell and folds its neck under in the shape of an "S". The side-necked turtle bends its neck to the side and hides it under the lip of the shell.

## ■ Figuring out a turtle's age

As a turtle grows, its shell grows, too. Every year a new ring of horny material forms around each scute. You can count these rings to figure out your turtle's age. But the rings get smooth and the age you come up with may not be exact.

● **To the Parent**

Of the 300 species of turtles in the world, about 20 have soft shells. Their carapaces are covered with a leathery skin rather than hard, horny shields. Soft-shelled turtles can be found in rivers and ponds. Their long necks and snorkel-like snouts let them breathe without surfacing. Soft-shelled turtles tend to be bad-tempered, which makes them poor pets for children.

# Why Do Snakes Shed Their Skin?

**ANSWER** A snake does not have the same kind of skin that a human has. As a snake grows, its skin gets too tight. The snake must get rid of, or shed, its old skin. Underneath is a new skin that fits the snake for a while. Then the snake will shed again.

## ■ Watch it shed

At shedding time a snake's skin turns cloudy white. Even the skin over its eyes turns white. First the dry, old skin comes off the tip of its face. Then the snake glides forward and brushes against objects that hold the old skin back. As the snake continues to slither, it slides out of its old skin, leaving it in one piece.

# Where Does a Pet Snake Live?

A glass tank is an ideal home for all the snakes pictured here. The tank must have a tight-fitting lid that lets in air. Place some newspapers or indoor-outdoor carpeting in the bottom of the tank. Pieces of bark or rocks will provide a safe place for your snake to hide.

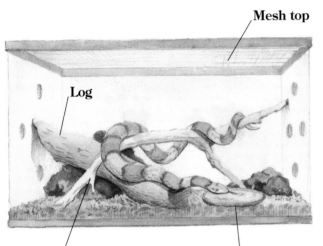

**Mesh top**

**Log**

**Tree branches**

**Water**

▶ **Rosy Boa**

A Boa Constrictor may be eight or nine feet long. A Rosy Boa is only three feet long. These gentle snakes make good pets.

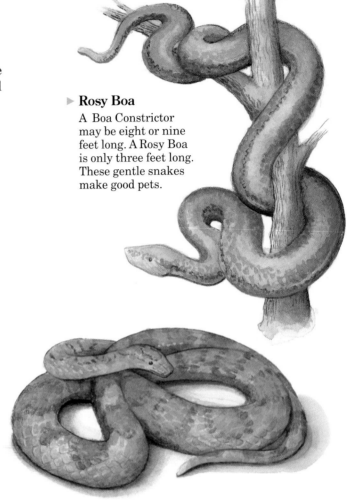

▲ **King Snake**

These snakes can grow twice as long as Rosy Boas and can be fighters. They are easy to spot because of their striped patterns.

### MINI-DATA

When you look at the skin that a snake has rubbed off, you may notice that the skin is inside out. To see why this is so, put on a sweater. Now take the sweater off by pulling it over your head. Like the snake's skin, your sweater comes off inside out as well.

▲ **Corn Snake**

The Corn Snake, or Red Rat Snake, is one of the most popular pet snakes. They are very tame and you can safely handle them. Pet Corn Snakes eat white mice that are raised as pet food.

● **To the Parent**

All snakes shed their skin many times during their lives. Young snakes double in size during their first year and therefore shed more frequently than older ones. A young snake may replace its skin every 45 days. Of the many types of snakes sold as pets, Corn snakes are among the most popular. They feed on defrosted mice that can be purchased at pet stores.

# Where Can a Pet Frog Live?

(ANSWER) Frogs live by rivers and ponds. Their eggs hatch in water. The little tadpoles live in the water until they turn into frogs. Then they must come out and breathe air. You can raise tadpoles at home until they become frogs. An aquarium, partly filled with water and some rocks above the water, makes a temporary home.

## ■ Collecting frog eggs

In the spring look for frog eggs at the edge of a pond. Scoop them out carefully. Collect some pond water including the green scum floating on top. Take some water plants, too.

# From tadpole to frog

A tadpole is born with a tail, but it has no legs. A tadpole has gills like fish for breathing in the water.

As the tadpole grows, it begins to change. First its back legs pop out and grow. Its front legs soon follow.

Finally the tail disappears. The gills are replaced by lungs. The frog comes up on land to breathe.

## ■ Making a home

Place the eggs, water, and plants in an aquarium. When the tadpoles hatch, they will swim in the water. The green scum you collected from the pond is their food. As they grow, try feeding them bits of lettuce.

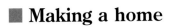

## ■ Releasing the frogs

When your tadpoles have grown into frogs, take them back to their pond. Always release them near the spot where you found them.

### ● To the Parent

Most frogs hatch from eggs as gill-breathing tadpoles. Slowly the structures needed for survival in the water are absorbed into the animals' body and replaced. This metamorphosis may take a month or longer depending on the species of frog. In spring and summer, children can find jellylike frog eggs attached to plants or rocks or floating in the water. Be sure to investigate local wildlife laws before collecting eggs, tadpoles, or adult frogs.

# ❓ What Is a Rodent?

ANSWER  Rodent is the name of a group of small, furry animals. The group includes mice, rats, guinea pigs, gerbils, and hamsters. All rodents have extralarge front teeth. They love to chew on things. Many rodents are playful and can be cared for easily, so they make excellent pets.

▼ **Hamster**
Many kinds of rodents live in large groups, but not hamsters. A pet hamster should always have a cage to itself.

▲ **Mouse**
Unlike their wild relatives, pet mice stay awake during much of the day and play. Some people buy two female mice so they can keep each other company.

▶ **Rat**
The rats raised to be pets are very gentle and smart. These friendly animals love to be held and petted.

◀ **Gerbil**

Gerbils are active and playful. They wrestle or chase each other around the cage. Their strong back legs make gerbils excellent jumpers, too.

▶ **Guinea pig**

Guinea pigs are friendly pets. They are a bit larger than other pet rodents. The animals are slow-moving and calm.

## ■ Rodent teeth

A rodent's front teeth keep growing for its entire life. Sometimes the animal must gnaw on hard things to grind them down, or the teeth will grow too long.

● **To the Parent**

There are more than 1,700 types of rodents found in the world. They are identified by pairs of prominent incisors. When properly aligned, a rodent's upper and lower incisors will keep each other worn down. If there is malocclusion, rodents chew wood and other hard objects to grind down their constantly growing teeth and to sharpen them. Many rodents thrive in captivity. That is one of the reasons why certain rodents make excellent first pets for young children.

# What Can a Pet Mouse or Rat Do?

**ANSWER** People think of these rodents as pests, but pet mice and rats are different from wild ones. They are clean animals and they are smart, too. These clever pets like to play with their owners. You can teach them simple tricks.

◄ **Rat**

► **Mouse**

▼ Make a maze out of wooden blocks. Place your pet rat at one end and food at the other. Watch your rat learn to find its way out.

A pet mouse learns to stay close to its owner. Put a bit of food in your pocket. The mouse will find it and snuggle inside the pocket.

## ■ More tricks and fun

A tame mouse likes to stay where it is warm. It will crawl up and down your shirt sleeve, tickling you as it goes. A tame rat will also know its owner. You can train your rat to climb up and sit on your shoulder.

## ■ If you lose your mouse

Here is a way to catch your mouse. Place its favorite food inside a tall glass jar. Build steps of blocks up to the top of the jar. Make sure all doors and windows in the room are shut. The mouse will climb the steps. Once it is in the jar it cannot get out.

● **To the Parent**

Rats and mice have always lived near people. In spite of our strong aversion to them, the ones bred to be pets are clean animals that are tame and intelligent. Through training they will learn to recognize their owner and perform simple tricks. Like many rodents bred as pets, mice and rats come in different colors with distinct markings. Be sure to choose young animals for pets, since they will usually adapt to a new home quickly and will be easier to train. Rats and mice are excellent first pets for children, because they are easy to care for and do not need a lot of space.

# How Did the Guinea Pig Get Its Name?

**ANSWER** This rodent came to us from the Guiana region in South America. Because guinea pigs grunt when they are hungry and sometimes squeak and squeal, people started to call them the pigs from Guiana. In time, people mispronounced the word Guiana and soon everybody started to call them guinea pigs.

▼ Guinea pigs can live in a tank or cage with a bottom that slides out for cleaning. At least three times per week they should be allowed out of their cage for play and exercise.

Oink! Oink!

Arf! Arf!

■ **A dog and a pig?**

Guinea pigs are not the only rodents named for another animal. Prairie dogs got their name because they live on the prairies and make a sound that reminds people of the barking of a dog.

# Why Do Some Guinea Pigs Have Such Strange Hair?

People have raised guinea pigs as pets for many years. When breeders came up with especially good-looking guinea pigs, they made sure those guinea pigs had many babies that would look like them. Soon there were special breeds as in cats and dogs.

▶ **Shorthaired**
This type of guinea pig has short fur that is soft and shiny. While some are one color, others have patterns of different color fur.

▼ **Peruvian**
Their long fur reaches from the middle of their back to the ground. Owners must comb the hair and keep it out of their pet's eyes.

▲ **Abyssinian**
These guinea pigs have swirling clusters of fur. Their long and wavy hair grows in clumps from certain spots all over their bodies. Abyssinian Guinea Pigs come in many different colors.

● **To the Parent**

Guinea pig is the popular name of the South American rodent called the cavy. Its origin from the Guiana region, combined with its slightly piglike grunts and squeals, may have been the reason for its unusual name. The guinea pig has a gentle disposition and is an excellent pet. Breeders have had dramatic success in developing guinea pigs with particular traits. Breeds include Himalayan, Angora, Agouti, and Shelties. Shorthaired guinea pigs are especially hardy pets. The more exotic longhaired breeds require greater dedication and care by their owners. All breeds need vitamin C supplements in their diets to avoid scurvy.

# Why Do Hamsters Have Such Big Cheeks?

**ANSWER** A tiny hamster's cheeks are its pockets. A wild hamster will stuff them with seeds and carry the food home. It stores the food in its underground burrow. A pet hamster often hides extra food in a corner of its cage to eat later.

▲ **Full pockets:** A pet hamster stuffs its cheeks with food to save until later.

## ■ Empty pockets

Hamster cheeks are covered with a loose layer of skin that contracts when empty. But the skin can stretch like a balloon to hold things.

## ■ Nursery pockets

Sometimes a hamster puts its babies in its cheek pouches. It can carry the babies from one place to another without hurting them.

**During the day**

Like many rodents, hamsters are nocturnal animals. That means they rest while the sun is up.

**At night**

At night hamsters get busy. They often have a wheel in their cage so they can get lots of exercise.

# Why Do Some Hamster Cages Look like Mazes?

Wild hamsters live in burrows in the ground. A single hamster digs many feet of tunnel space for its home. Sometimes the owner of a pet hamster puts together plastic tubes. The hamster likes to run through these tubes as if they were tunnels in a burrow.

▼ A hamster's underground burrow has tunnels plus rooms for sleeping, storing seeds, and going to the bathroom.

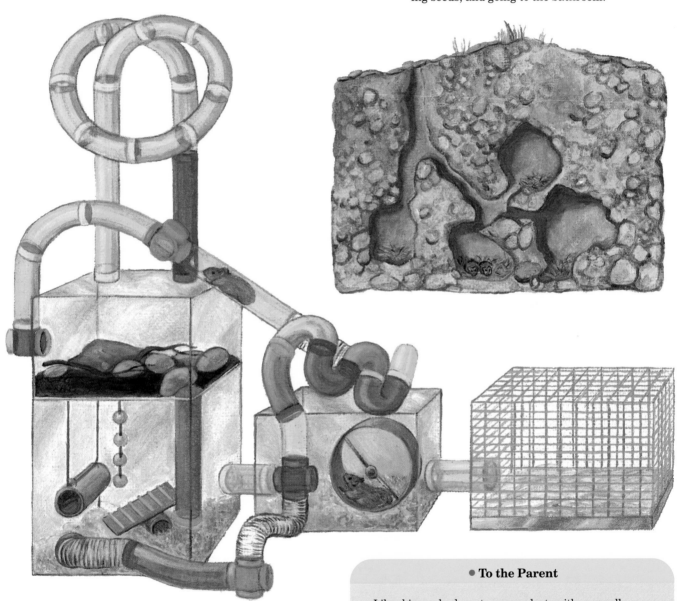

▲ Hamster owners connect a maze of tubes and then watch their pet scurry from one place to another. Sometimes the tubes run to separate tanks like the chambers in a wild hamster burrow.

## ● To the Parent

Like chipmunks, hamsters are rodents with unusually large cheek pouches for transporting food. In the wild, hamsters are very active. They may travel as much as five miles at night in search of food. For a pet hamster an exercise wheel inside its cage is essential. A system of plastic tunnels specially designed for hamsters provides a fascinating view of their burrow life. When building an elaborate setup for a hamster, pet owners must take care. These little rodents are known for their ability to push through small spaces and escape from their cages.

# Why Do Rabbits Thump Their Feet?

**ANSWER** In the wild, rabbits thump their feet against the ground to warn each other of danger. Pet rabbits still do this to signal that someone is coming. Sometimes they want to let the others know that they are mad about something.

# ■ Rabbit or hare?

▲ **Rabbit**
Rabbits live underground in burrows called warrens. Hares live in shallow nests in the ground.

▲ **Hare**
Most hares have bigger ears than rabbits. Thanks to their longer legs they run faster, too.

# ■ Different pet breeds

▶ **Lop ear**
These rabbits have long ears that bend and fall to the side. Lop ears come in many different colors.

▼ **Angora**
These medium-size rabbits have fur that is more than three inches long, wavy, and wonderfully soft.

▲ **New Zealand White**
This gentle white rabbit has a strange name: It was bred in the United States, not in New Zealand.

### ● To the Parent

Although they resemble rodents in some ways, rabbits and hares are members of the order Lagomorpha. These prolific breeding animals are found in most parts of the world. Unlike hares, wild rabbits are social animals. They dig elaborate burrows, where they live in groups of a dozen or so animals. A wild rabbit's thumping is a warning understood by other rabbits. The same communication can be seen in pet rabbits. Veterinarians note that rabbits thump after having their teeth trimmed and their ears cleaned.

# Can Rabbits Be Housebroken?

**ANSWER** Wild rabbits are clean animals. In their underground burrows, called warrens, they have a separate room where they go to the bathroom. Pet rabbits are clean animals, too. That is one reason why they can be housebroken. They can learn to use a litter box, just as cats do.

## ■ How to train your rabbit

Place a litter box—the kind made for cats—where your rabbit will find it. Make sure it is not too far from its cage.

Fill the box with cat litter. You may need to experiment with different kinds to see which type of litter your rabbit likes best.

At first you must gently set your rabbit in the litter box. You may place a few of its droppings in the box, so the rabbit will understand what to do. Repeat this often until your rabbit learns to use the box.

You can teach your rabbit other things, too. If a rabbit starts nibbling on houseplants or mistakes the soil in the planter for a litter box, stamp your foot and say "No!"

# Should a Rabbit Live Inside or Out?

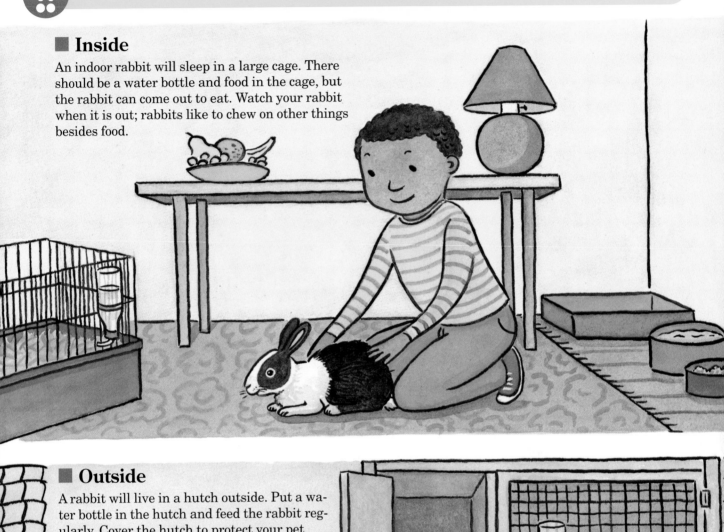

## ■ Inside
An indoor rabbit will sleep in a large cage. There should be a water bottle and food in the cage, but the rabbit can come out to eat. Watch your rabbit when it is out; rabbits like to chew on other things besides food.

## ■ Outside
A rabbit will live in a hutch outside. Put a water bottle in the hutch and feed the rabbit regularly. Cover the hutch to protect your pet from bad weather and wild animals.

● **To the Parent**

When living indoors a rabbit can learn to use a litter box. It can also be trained to respond to other simple commands. Stamping your foot will often get a rabbit to stop doing something it should not do. As in the wild, this thumping noise is a warning signal that will get the animal's attention. If you keep a pet rabbit outside, make sure its hutch is roomy and safe from bad weather and wild animals. In hot weather, the hutch must be in the shade. Some ice cubes or a frozen milk carton will provide needed relief in the hutch.

# Why Do Ferrets Smell So Bad?

**ANSWER** A ferret belongs to a family of animals that includes skunks, badgers, and weasels. An excited ferret gives off a strong smell. But ferrets do not smell as bad as skunks do. They are playful animals that make great pets. Their relatives shown at bottom are not good to keep as pets.

Hob   Kit   Jill

▲ A baby ferret is called a kit. The mother is called a jill and the father is known as a hob.

► Ferret

## ■ Relatives of the ferret

▼ **Skunk**
When disturbed or frightened, skunks will lift their tail and send out a horrible-smelling spray. This mist may travel as far as 10 feet.

▲ **Badger**
The badger is larger and its body is shaped more like that of a skunk than a ferret. Badgers live in burrows that they dig with their sharp front claws.

# Is a Pet Ferret More like a Cat or a Dog?

## ▲ Doglike behavior

Sometimes a ferret acts like a dog. The ferret will come running if you call its name, and it can be trained to do simple tricks. One pet ferret living on a farm was known to play chase with a horse, just as a dog might.

## ▼ Catlike behavior

In some ways a ferret is like a cat. It can be trained to use a litter box. A ferret is playful like a kitten and will push a ball around with its nose.

**CHECK IT OUT**

Ferrets are curious pets. Their slim body allows them to squeeze into narrow places and to explore.

## ▶ Weasel

Weasels have slender bodies. They are very intelligent. They hunt small animals including rodents and rabbits.

## • To the Parent

Ferrets have a history of domesticity that may date back to ancient Egyptian times. Pet ferrets have been bred from a European strain of the animal as opposed to the endangered Black-Footed Ferret of North America. Like all weasels, ferrets produce a strong smell from an anal scent gland. Pet ferrets usually have their scent gland removed. They must also be neutered to reduce their musky odor. Ferrets are highly social animals that get along well with people, cats, and dogs. Parents of infants should be warned, however, that some ferrets have attacked sleeping babies.

#  Can an Insect Be a Pet?

**ANSWER** Insects are fun to watch. Certain harmless ones like ants, crickets, and caterpillars can sometimes be kept as pets. Like any other pet, these tiny creatures need the right kind of home.

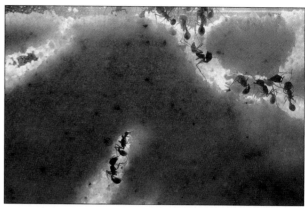

▲ An ant nest is a series of tunnels in the ground. Pet ants are kept in an ant farm where you can see the tunnels and watch the busy ants running about.

## ■ Making an ant farm

**1** To make an ant farm, start with an empty glass tank. Carefully cover the sides of your tank with black paper to make the ants think they're inside the earth.

**2** Collect ants in the yard or park. Look for them under stones in the damp soil. Dig into the ground with a spade to find them in their tunnels.

**3** Place your ants in the tank. Fill it with moist soil. Add some leaves and bits of fruit. Make sure the lid fits tight.

**4** After a few days remove the black paper from the sides. Can you see the tunnels that the ants built?

# ■ A home for a cricket or caterpillar

An insect pet needs a simple terrarium that you can make. Fill a jar with plants and soil from your garden. Then look for insects such as crickets or caterpillars.

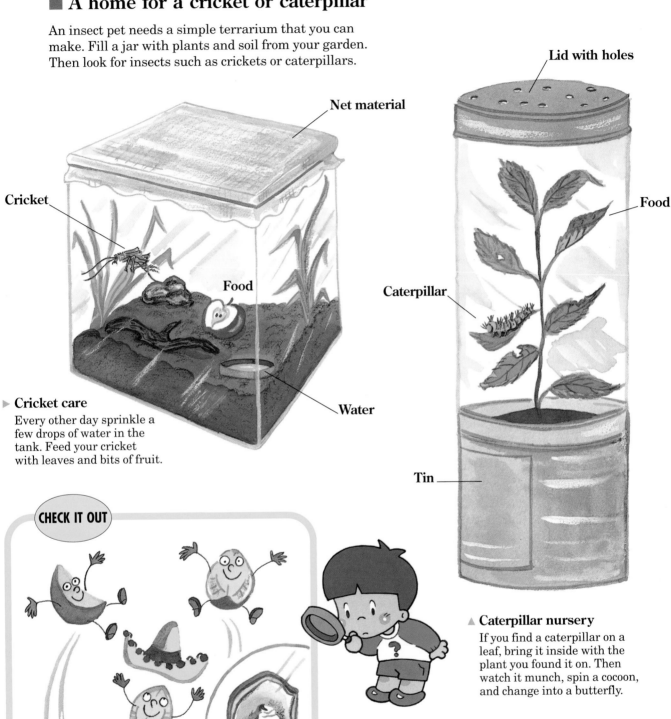

Net material

Lid with holes

Cricket

Food

Food

Caterpillar

Water

Tin

▶ **Cricket care**

Every other day sprinkle a few drops of water in the tank. Feed your cricket with leaves and bits of fruit.

**CHECK IT OUT**

**Mexican Jumping Bean**

This is really an insect pet. Inside the bean is the larva of a codling moth. When you turn the bean upside down, the larva will turn it back.

▲ **Caterpillar nursery**

If you find a caterpillar on a leaf, bring it inside with the plant you found it on. Then watch it munch, spin a cocoon, and change into a butterfly.

● **To the Parent**

Ant farms can be made from small aquarium tanks with tight-fitting lids. Commercial ant farms are sold in pet stores and hobby shops. In many cases, after purchasing the materials, the buyer receives the ants (complete with queen) by mail. Some insects such as caterpillars, crickets, and grasshoppers can be kept as pets in terrariums. When the caterpillar turns into a butterfly and the cricket has chirped its song for a few days, you should return these insects to their natural home.

# Why Can't You Make a Pet Out of a Wild Animal?

 **ANSWER** Some animals are raised to be pets. They would have a hard time living without people. But wild animals are different from tame ones: They must be on their own. If you tried to make a pet out of a wild animal, it might scratch or bite you. The frightened animal would not be happy and neither would you.

## ■ A fox in search of food

In winter when there is a lot of snow on the ground, some wild animals will come close to the house looking for something to eat. This fox may seem friendly, but you should not pet it. The fox may be sick with rabies or some other disease. So, keep your distance.

# ■ Always watch from a distance

The best spot to watch wildlife is from a safe place. Some animals live closer than you might think. Raccoons like to pick through garbage. Look for them at night.

◀ If you see a wild animal that seems injured, watch it carefully but don't get close. It may get up and go on its way. If you think the animal needs help, ask a parent to call a local animal shelter or a veterinarian for advice. You can find their numbers in the telephone book.

### ● To the Parent

While there are certainly exceptions, children should keep their distance from most wild animals. If a wild mammal is acting as if it is tame, be extremely cautious. This is an example of abnormal behavior and could be a sign of rabies. Raccoons, skunks, foxes, and bats are some of the mammals that have been known to carry the disease. Should you come upon an injured or orphaned wild animal, it is best to seek the help of an expert. Look up the name of the local fish and wildlife department, or seek the help of knowledgeable people at zoos or nature centers.

# ? Can an Animal Have a Pet?

**ANSWER** Most pets belong to people, but a pet gorilla named Koko has her own pet. Koko has been raised by scientists. She speaks using sign language. When her keeper asked her what she wanted for her birthday, she signed "cat." Sometime later Koko got a kitten. She named her pet All Ball. When All Ball was run over by a car, Koko cried. Now she has a new kitten. She calls it Red.

## ■ Koko and her pets

Koko likes to play games with her pet kitten. She blows in the kitten's face and wants it to blow back at her. Her favorite games are chase and tickle. She brushes the kitten and carries it on her back and shoulders the way gorilla mothers do with their babies.

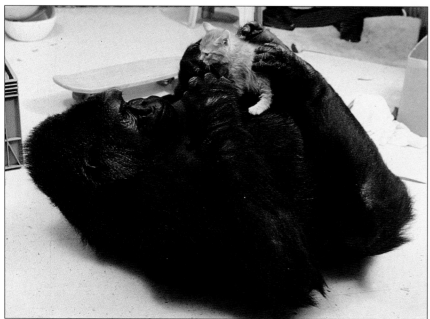

▲ Koko likes to hug her kitten, Red, and cradle it on her legs like a gorilla baby.

▲ Koko picked out her first kitten from a litter of three. She chose a gray, striped Manx kitten, without a tail, and named it All Ball.

78

# Can Pets Be Friends?

Whether different pets can be friends depends on the kinds of pets. Some animals like to live together in large groups. They often get along with other animals if they are not frightened by them. When putting together different animals, it is always wise to be careful. Do not leave them alone unless you are absolutely certain both animals will be safe.

▲ Guinea pigs and rabbits get along and sometimes live together.

### ▲ Dogs and cats

Dogs and cats are thought of as natural enemies, but that is not always the case. When dogs and cats are raised in the same house, they can be good friends. This works best when they first meet as kittens and puppies, when they are not yet set in their ways.

● **To the Parent**

Koko has been raised by Dr. Katherine Patterson of the Gorilla Foundation. Koko communicates using American Sign Language. All Ball was her first kitten. Like all cat fanciers, Koko displayed great warmth and affection toward her pet. She was very upset when All Ball was hit by a car and died. Sometime later she received another cat that she named Red. Many other animals are highly social and thrive with this kind of companionship. Caution is always advised when placing two animals of different species (or even two of the same species) together.

# What Kinds of Pets Are These?

◄ **Marbled salamander**

This strange-looking salamander is a relative of lizards. It has no scales to protect its skin and must live in water to stay moist. Salamanders breathe through their bushy external gills.

► **Tarantula**

The hairy tarantula is bigger than a hand. Its bite is poisonous to some animals, but not to people. Tarantulas can be kept as pets in a glass tank, equipped with water and food and a heat lamp.

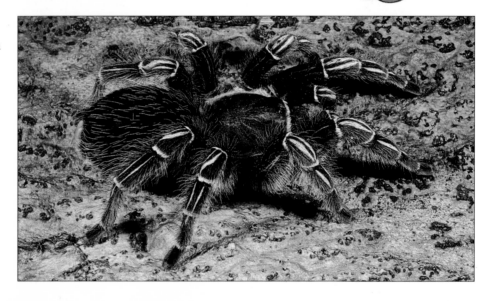

◄ **Frog**

Almost hidden from view, this bullfrog peers out of the water with bulging eyes. The best home for a pet frog is a backyard pond.

● **To the Parent**

Keeping any of these animals as pets in a home requires a fair amount of time and devotion. They need special care and must be housed and fed properly. A frog can live in an aqua-terrarium that is roughly half land and half water. The salamander needs an aquarium, and the tarantula thrives in a desertlike environment.

# Growing-Up Album

What's Wrong with This? ...................................82
Help These Animals Get Home ......................84
Pin the Tail on the Pet ..................................86

# What's Wrong with This?

These animals act funny. They all do things they could not do in real life. Can you tell what's wrong?

Fish

Dog

Frog

Birds

**Turtle**

**Rabbits**

**Cat**

Answers: A fish cannot ride a hamster wheel. A dog cannot walk a fence like a cat can. A frog does not eat a bone. Birds do not play kickball. A turtle cannot run fast enough to chase a mouse. Rabbits cannot climb trees. A cat will not catch a stick.

# Help These Animals Get Home

These pets have lost the way to their homes. Can you tell where they should go and which home belongs to whom? Write the right number in each square.

1. Fish

2. Rabbit

3. Dog

4. Hamster

5. Bird

6. Lizard

A ⬚

B ⬚

C ⬚

D ⬚

E ⬚

F ⬚

Answers: E-1; D-2; B-3; F-4; C-5; A-6

85

# Pin the Tail on the Pet

Pet tails come in many different sizes and shapes. Can you match the tail with each pet? Place the right number in each square.

A

B

D

E

G

C

F

H

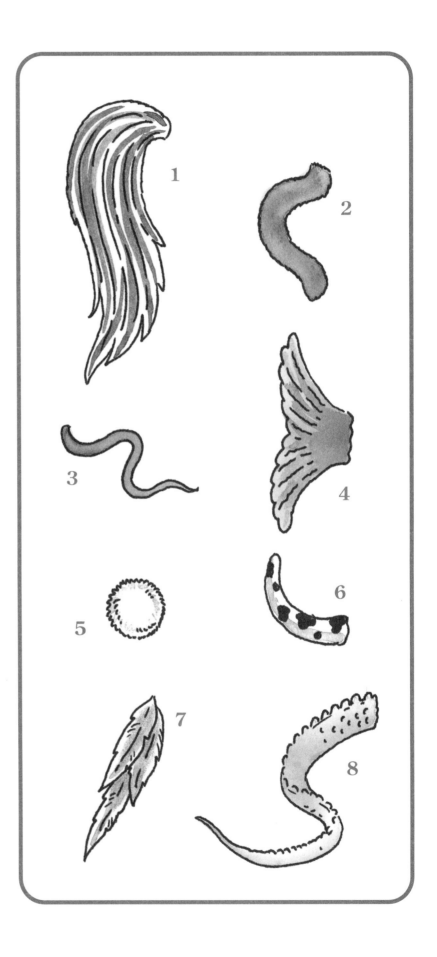

1

2

3

4

5

6

7

8

Answers: A-4; B-1; C-3; D-8; E-2; F-7; G-6; H-5

Time-Life Books is a division of Time Life Inc.

TIME LIFE INC.

PRESIDENT and CEO: George Artandi

TIME-LIFE BOOKS

PRESIDENT: John D. Hall
PUBLISHER/MANAGING EDITOR: Neil Kagan

A Child's First Library of Learning
PETS

EDITOR: Karin Kinney
DIRECTOR, NEW PRODUCT DEVELOPMENT: Elizabeth D. Ward
MARKETING DIRECTOR: Wendy A. Foster

*Associate Editor/Research and Writing:* Teresa Graham
*Marketing Manager:* Janine Wilkin
*Picture Coordinator:* David A. Herod
*Picture Researcher:* Mary M. Saxton

*Design:* Studio A—Antonio Alcalá, Sue Dowdall, Virginia Ibarra-Garza, Wendy Schleicher
*Special Contributors:* Andrew Gutelle, Susan Perry (research and writing); Barbara Klein (overread); Colette Stockum (copyedit).

*Consultants:* Peter Farrell, DMV, is the director of Del Ray Animal Hospital in Alexandria, Va. Scott Stahl, DMV, is a veterinarian at Pender Veterinary Clinic in Fairfax, Va.

*Correspondents:* Maria Vincenza Aloisi (Paris), Christine Hinze (London), Christina Lieberman (New York).

*Vice President, Director of Finance:* Christopher Hearing
*Vice President, Book Production:* Marjann Caldwell
*Director of Operations:* Eileen Bradley
*Director of Photography and Research:* John Conrad Weiser
*Director of Editorial Administration:* Judith W. Shanks
*Production Manager:* Marlene Zack
*Quality Assurance Manager:* James King
*Library:* Louise D. Forstall

*Photography:* Cover: © Comstock, Inc. Back cover: © Photodisc, Inc. Title page: © PhotoDisc, Inc. 7: © Sygma. 12: © Jane Burton/Bruce Coleman, Inc. (3)—© Margaret Miller/Photo Researchers (3). 13: Kit Houghton, Spaxton, Somerset (3). 15: © Richard Hutchings, The National Audubon Society Collection/Photo Researchers. 21: © Tom Nebbia/The Stock Market; © Lawrence Migdale, The National Audubon Society Collection/Photo Researchers. 30: © Jane Burton/Bruce Coleman, Inc. 33: Agence Nature/NHPA, Ardingly, Sussex; Scala/Art Resource, New York. 35: Tom Nebbia. 40: © Robert Bornemann, The National Audubon Society Collection/Photo Researchers. 44: © M. H. Sharp/Photo Researchers. 53: © Miriam Austerman/Animals Animals. 56: © Jeff Lepore, The National Audubon Society Collection/Photo Researchers—© John Serrao, The National Audubon Society Collection/ Photo Researchers. 58: © Jack Dermid/Bruce Coleman, Inc. 61: Jerome Wexler. 66: Jerome Wexler. 69: © Leonard Lee Rue III/Animals Animals; © Robert Mailer/Animals Animals. 74: © S. L. Craig, Jr./Bruce Coleman, Inc. 76: © PhotoDisc, Inc. 78: Dr. Ronald H. Cohn/The Gorilla Foundation. 80: © Stephen Dalton/Animals Animals—© James Rowan/Tony Stone Images—© Matt Meadows/Peter Arnold, Inc.

*Illustrations:* Loel Barr: 9, 13, 14-15, 18 **(middle)**, 31, 32 **(bottom)**, 36, 37 **(bottom left)**, 56 **(top right)**, 57 **(bottom left)**, 63, 79, 82-87; Leila Cabib: 10 **(upper right)**, 20 **(upper right)**, 25 **(top left)**, 74-75; Robin DeWitt: 34-35, 48-49, 50 **(bottom)**, 51, 60-61, 64 **(top right)**, 65, 66 **(middle)**;

Linda Greigg: 19 **(top & middle)**, 22 **(top & middle)**, 23 **(top & middle)**, 26 **(top & middle)**, 27 **(top)**, 37 **(middle)**, 44-45, 50 **(top right)**, 62, 70, 73 **(top left & right)**; Lili Robins: 4-5, 8 **(bottom)**, 24-25, 39 **(top 4)**, 57 **(top 3)**, 72-73 **(middle & bottom)**; Carol Schwartz: 10-11, 16-27 **(bottom)**, 40-41, 42-43, 77; Bethann Thornburgh: 6-7, 8 **(top)**, 18 **(top)**, 32 **(top)**, 46-47, 53, 54 **(top)**, 64 **(bottom)**, 71, 72 **(top)**, 73 **(lower right)**; Bobbi Tull: 28-29, 39, 68-69; Jeanne Turner: 20-21 **(middle)**, 37 **(top)**, 38 **(top)**, 52, 54-55, 58-59, 67; Chris Young: 38 **(middle & bottom)**.

TIME-LIFE is a trademark of Time Warner Inc. U.S.A.

**Library of Congress Cataloging-in-Publication Data**
Pets.
     p. cm.—(A Child's First Library of Learning)
    Summary: Explores the world of pets, providing information on animal characteristics and behavior in question and answer format.
    ISBN 0-8094-9478-7
    1. Pets—Miscellanea—Juvenile literature. 2. Animals—Miscellanea—Juvenile literature. [1. Pets—Miscellanea. 2. Animals—Miscellanea. 3. Questions and answers.] I. Time-Life Books. II. Series.
SF416.2.P475 1996
636.088'7—dc20
                              96-15197
                                  CIP
                                  AC

OTHER PUBLICATIONS:

| COOKING | DO IT YOURSELF |
|---|---|
| Weight Watchers₀ Smart Choice Recipe Collection | The Time-Life Complete Gardener |
| | Home Repair and Improvement |
| Great Taste–Low Fat | The Art of Woodworking |
| Williams-Sonoma Kitchen Library | Fix It Yourself |

| TIME-LIFE KIDS | HISTORY |
|---|---|
| Family Time Bible Stories | The American Story |
| Library of First Questions and Answers | Voices of the Civil War |
| A Child's First Library of Learning | The American Indians |
| I Love Math | Lost Civilizations |
| Nature Company Discoveries | Mysteries of the Unknown |
| Understanding Science & Nature | Time Frame |
| | The Civil War |
| SCIENCE/NATURE | Cultural Atlas |
| Voyage Through the Universe | |

For information on and a full description of any of the Time-Life Books series listed above, please call 1-800-621-7026 or write:

Reader Information
Time-Life Customer Service
P.O. Box C-32068
Richmond, Virginia 23261-2068